God's Plan for Your MONEY

Other Whitaker House Titles
by Derek Prince

God's Plan for Your MONEY

Derek Prince

WHITAKER HOUSE

GOD'S PLAN FOR YOUR MONEY

Derek Prince Ministries–International
P.O. Box 19501
Charlotte, NC 287219
www.dpmusa.org

ISBN: 0-88368-707-0
Printed in the United States of America
© 1995 by Derek Prince Ministries–International

Whitaker House
30 Hunt Valley Circle
New Kensington, PA 15068
www.whitakerhouse.com

Library of Congress Cataloging-in-Publication Data

Prince, Derek.
God's plan for your money / by Derek Prince.
p. cm.
ISBN 0-88368-707-0 (pbk.)
1. Stewardship, Christian.   2. Money—Religious aspects—
Christianity.   3. Finance, Personal—Religious aspects—
Christianity. I. Title.
BV772 .P75 2001
241'.68—dc21
2001004219

2 3 4 5 6 7 8 9 10 11 12 / 11 10 09 08 07 06 05 04 03

Contents

God's All-Inclusive Plan

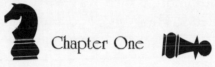

Chapter One

God's All-Inclusive Plan

Y ou may be surprised to learn that God has a plan for your money. You may have the idea that money is too sordid for spiritual people. Like some of us, you may have grown up with a religious background that referred to money as "filthy lucre." However, this is not a biblical view of money.

In contemporary culture, money plays a large role in each of our lives. If God does not have a plan for our money, then a major part of our lives is not under His control. In turn, this circumstance will inevitably affect other areas of our lives. The truth is that many Christians, whose lives are not really under God's control, try to

God's Plan for Your Money

solve their problems by becoming more spiritual. However, many times the answer is to be more practical.

If you are not handling your finances in line with God's plan, then your whole life is out of joint. No matter how spiritual you may be in other areas, you will never know the real blessing and overruling of God in your life until you bring your money into line with the will of God as revealed in His Word. You see, the Bible clearly reveals that God does have a plan for our money.

As a teacher of God's Word, it is my responsibility to share with you God's plan for your money just as I would share His plan for any other area of your life. In Acts Paul said this:

20 You know that I have not hesitated to preach anything that would be helpful to you but have taught you publicly and from house to house.

27 For I have not hesitated to proclaim to you the whole will of God. (Acts 20:20, 27)

In other words, Paul was saying that he had declared to them the *"whole will of God,"* and that he had taught everything in the Word of God that would be helpful to God's people. The whole will of God includes His will for our money. It is part of the total counsel or plan of God.

I want to point out in a general way that God really does have a plan that covers every area of our lives. In Romans, Paul said:

God's All-Inclusive Plan

¹Therefore, I urge you, brothers, in view of God's mercy, to offer your bodies as living sacrifices, holy and pleasing to God—this is your spiritual act of worship. (Romans 12:1)

Notice that spiritual worship includes our bodies; it moves right into the physical world. Some people think the body is not spiritual. Being spiritual includes doing the right thing with your body—presenting it to God as a living sacrifice. Paul continued in the next verse,

²Do not conform any longer to the pattern of this world, but be transformed by the renewing of your mind. Then you will be able to test and approve what God's will is—his good, pleasing and perfect will. (v. 12:2)

God's will is unfolded in three successive phases by three beautiful words. The will of God is *"good, pleasing* [or *"acceptable"* KJV] *and perfect."* These three words represent three phases in our perception of the will of God.

When we first begin to perceive God's will, we discover that it is good. God never wants anything bad for any of His people. Then we learn that His will is pleasing or acceptable. The more we perceive it, the more we want to embrace it. Finally, as we move on in the perception and the application of God's will, we realize that it is perfect or complete. The whole, complete will of God covers all areas of your life—and that includes your money.

God's Plan for Your Money

Paul pointed out two essential steps to finding God's will. First, surrender yourself without reservation to God. Paul said to place your body on God's altar *as a living sacrifice* (Romans 12:1). He was comparing the body with the Old Testament sacrifices in which the animals that were offered were first killed and then placed on the altar. In this manner they were set apart for God. Paul said that you must do the same with your body: put it on the altar of God's service without reservation. The only difference is that you do not kill the body, but rather present it as a living sacrifice.

The second essential step to finding God's will is learning to think God's way. Paul called it being renewed in your mind. This means changing your whole outlook, including the way you think, your values, your standards, and your priorities. Only as your mind is renewed can you perceive what is God's will.

I want to point out something else about your money that is very important. Do not underestimate your money, belittle it, or think it is unspiritual or unimportant. What does your money really represent? I suggest that it represents four very important aspects of you: your time, your strength, your talents, and, quite possibly, your inheritance.

Your inheritance may be money or other valuable things, like houses or lands, which were passed on to you from people who loved and cared for you when their lives came to an end. Perhaps you went to college and had a fairly elaborate education. All those years of education are represented by your money because if you did not have the education, you could not make the money that you do. Or you might have special talents or abilities that are not in the academic field, that are more practical in nature. Those talents and abilities are represented in your money. Certainly, too, your money represents your time. If you work eight hours a day, five days a week, that is forty hours of your life invested in the money you earn.

When you invest your money, you are investing a major part of yourself for good or bad. I hope you can begin to see how important it is that you invest yourself through your money in that which is good and in accordance with God's will and plan.

God's plan for your life, including your money, is summed up in one beautiful word: *prosperity.* This idea is stated in 3 John, where the writer said to a fellow Christian,

> *[2]Beloved, I pray that in all respects you may prosper and be in good health, just as your soul prospers.* (3 John 2:2 NAS)

Notice that the key word in this verse is *"prosper."* It covers three areas: your soul, your

God's Plan for Your Money

physical health, and your finances or material needs. In each area the revealed will of God is prosperity or success. God wants you to succeed in the area of your soul, in the area of your physical body, and in the area of your finances.

Failure, defeat, frustration, and poverty are not the will of God. I grew up in a religious tradition where being holy meant you had to be poor. I respect people who hold that view, but it is not a scriptural one.

God or Mammon?

Chapter Two

God ^{or} Mammon?

We need to see that our personal attitudes toward money are very important. This truth can be stated as the following principle:

Your attitude toward money actually reveals your attitude toward God Himself.

I want to quote to you the words of Jesus on the subject. In the Sermon on the Mount, we find that Jesus stated the following about this topic:

God's Plan for Your Money

24 No one can serve two masters; for either he will hate the one and love the other, or he will hold to one and despise the other. You cannot serve God and mammon. (Matthew 6:24 NAS)

First, let us look for a moment at the meaning of the word *"mammon."* The *New International translation* says, *"You cannot serve both God and money,"* but that does not fully express the meaning of the word, because mammon is more than just money. Mammon is an evil, spiritual power that grips men and enslaves them through the medium of money. Mammon is not money itself, but the spiritual power that works in the world and the lives of millions of people through their attitudes toward money.

Jesus said that you cannot serve God and mammon. Then He said, *"Either* [you] *will hate the one and love the other, or* [you] *will hold to one and despise the other."* In each case, Jesus naturally put God first and mammon second. Either you will hate God and love mammon, or you will hold onto God and despise mammon. That is a serious thought. If you love mammon, you hate God. On the other hand, if you hold onto God and your life is committed to Him, you will despise mammon. This attitude is not hating money, but loathing that satanic force that enslaves men and women through money. You will detest it, and you will not let it dominate you. You cannot maintain a position of neutrality on this subject. We must acknowledge in our lives the claim of one or the other. It is not a choice of whether we

God or Mammon?

will serve; it is a choice only of whom we will serve—either God or mammon.

Jesus said that it is a question of priorities:

> *33 But seek first His [God's] kingdom and His righteousness; and all these things shall be added to you.*　　　(Matthew 6:33 NAS)

Jesus did not say we have to be without *"these things,"* but He says we must not put these things first. We must put the kingdom of God and His righteousness first in our lives on a consistent basis—that is, commitment to God, His kingdom, and His purposes. Jesus said that if we do not run after mammon and make it our god, but if we serve the true God and seek His kingdom and righteousness, then God will see to it that all the material and financial things we need are added to us.

Pursuing money is such an awful strain and leads to so much frustration. Do not chase after money. That is what Jesus says. Let money pursue you. If you have followed the right course in your life, then the money will be added to you. You do not have to lie awake at night or spend hours hatching plans to get rich.

Having followed that principle for more than forty years, by the grace of God I can attest that God is faithful. Sometimes my faith has been tested. Sometimes I have had to deny myself things that the world esteems very highly. But, as

God's Plan for Your Money

I look back at all I have gone through, I have to say God has been totally faithful.

The principle of putting God first runs all the way through the Bible. In the third chapter of Proverbs, we find two beautiful verses that say the same thing:

> *9 Honor the LORD with your wealth, with the firstfruits of all your crops;*
>
> *10 then your barns will be filled to overflowing, and your vats will brim over with new wine.*
> (Proverbs 3:9–10)

The *"barns"* and the *"vats"* are all of your material needs. They will be abundantly supplied and will overflow when you honor God with your wealth. The way in which you honor God with your wealth is by giving Him the *"firstfruits."* This means setting aside the first (or best) portion for God. We either honor or dishonor God with our money. There is no neutral ground.

Let me say, lovingly, that God does not want your tips! When the offering plate comes around at church, do not drop a quarter in. That is insulting God. As a matter of fact, for most people today, giving a dollar is an insult to God. You would slip a dollar into the hand of the restaurant parking lot valet who parks your car. Do not treat God like that, because you are insulting and dishonoring Him. Similarly, the Scripture points out that putting money ahead of God is also idolatry:

God or Mammon?

> *⁵Therefore put to death your members which are on the earth: fornication, uncleanness, passion, evil desire, and covetousness, which is idolatry.*　(Colossians 3:5 NKJV)

Notice that Paul said covetousness is idolatry. When you seek money first, you are making money your god, which is rightly called idolatry. The Lord said to Israel, *"Thou shalt have none other gods before me* [or *"besides Me"* AMP]" (Deuteronomy 5:7 KJV). In our contemporary culture, far more people have made money their god rather than the true God. They are guilty of idolatry.

Notice that in Colossians Paul put covetousness side by side with many other unpleasant things such as fornication and uncleanness. Most churches would not accept people who live in fornication (sexual immorality), but, frankly, our churches are full of people who are guilty of covetousness and idolatry.

Another Scripture, 1 Timothy 6:9–10, carries a warning against making money your God and desiring to be rich:

> *⁹ But those who desire to be rich fall into temptation and a snare, and into many foolish and harmful lusts which drown men in destruction and perdition.*

> *¹⁰ For the love of money is a root of all kinds of evil* [money is not evil; the love of money is],

God's Plan for Your Money

for which some have strayed from the faith in their greediness [or covetousness], *and pierced themselves through with many sorrows.*

(1 Timothy 6:9–10 NKJV)

Now here is the remedy or alternative:

11But you, O man of God, flee these things [covetousness, love of money, materialism] *and pursue righteousness, godliness, faith, love, patience, gentleness.* (1 Timothy 6:11 NKJV)

No vacuum can exist in our lives. If we are to be clear of the love of money, we must pursue something else. Something else must take its place. Paul said, *"Pursue righteousness, godliness, faith, love, patience, gentleness."*

Faith is necessary to break the control of mammon in your life. At some point or other, you are going to have to do something to release yourself from the domination of mammon.

Personally, I can look back on a point in my life when I gave to the Lord's work everything I owned financially and materially. I gave up a prestigious, well-paying job with a tremendous future and stepped out in naked faith with nothing to uphold me but the promises of God. When I did so, the control of mammon over my life was broken. I refused to be a slave of mammon.

Offering Is Part of Worship

Chapter Three

Offering Is Part of Worship

God wants us to see our money as something holy that we offer in worship to Him, and that without this offering our worship is incomplete. We will start with examples from the Old Testament.

In Exodus 23:14–15, God gave regulations for every male among the children of Israel to come up to Jerusalem three times a year. They were to offer worship and to celebrate before God in the temple. Here is part of the regulation He gave:

> *14 Three times a year you are to celebrate a festival to me.*

God's Plan for Your Money

15 Celebrate the Feast of Unleavened Bread; for seven days eat bread made without yeast, as I commanded you. Do this at the appointed time in the month of Abib, for in that month you came out of Egypt. No one is to appear before Me empty-handed. (Exodus 23:14–15)

"No one is to appear before Me empty-handed."

This was part of God's ordinance for worship and celebration in the temple. Israel had to come up at God's appointed time and in God's appointed way, and no Israelite was to appear before Him empty-handed. Every Israelite had to have an offering for God as part of the celebration and worship.

In Psalm 96:8–9 the psalmist said to all of God's people,

*8 Give to the LORD the glory due His name;
Bring an offering and come into His courts.*

9 Oh, worship the LORD in the beauty of holiness!
(NKJV)

The Scripture says, *"Bring an offering and come into His courts,"* but do not come without an offering. Here are three important facts about the offering of finances, or anything else, to God.

1)   Bringing an offering gives glory to God. The psalmist said, *"Give to the Lord the glory due His name; Bring an offering."* How are we to give glory to God? By bringing an offering.

26

Offering Is Part of Worship

2) Bringing an offering gives us access to God's courts. We have no right to claim access to God if we do not come with an offering. In Exodus 23:15, God said, *"No one is to appear before me emptyhanded."* If you want to appear before God and come into His courts, you must bring an offering.

3) Bringing an offering is a God-appointed part of our worship. The psalmist continued, *"Oh, worship the LORD in the beauty of holiness!"* (Psalm 96:9). This tells us that our worship is not complete until we bring our offerings to God.

We saw earlier that when we give our money to God, we are giving a very important part of our lives. We are giving Him our time, our strength, and our talents. Most of us put the major portion of our efforts into the work that brings our income. When we offer God the appointed share of our income, we are offering ourselves to God. And there is nothing more holy we can offer to God than ourselves.

God says, in effect, "If you want to come into My courts, to appear before Me, to give glory to Me, and to worship Me in the beauty of holiness, then bring your offering." Bringing an offering, worship, and holiness are all very closely connected in God's plan for our lives.

Another important point that many of God's people do not fully understand is that God keeps a record of what His people offer. God has an account book for every one of us. To illustrate this truth, we need to read the seventh chapter of Numbers.

This chapter describes what the twelve princes of the tribes of Israel offered to God. Each prince offered exactly the same, yet each of their offerings is described in detail, item by item. God did not say, "The second prince offered the same as the first," or, "All twelve princes each offered this." Rather, the record goes through every item in the offering of each prince. The Bible is a very economical book in that it does not waste any space. When God enumerated identical offerings in this passage, He was illustrating for us how very carefully He records what we offer to Him. Here is the account of the first prince:

10 When the altar was anointed, the leaders [or princes] *brought their offerings for its dedication and presented them before the altar.*

11 For the LORD had said to Moses, "Each day one leader is to bring his offering for the dedication of the altar." [For twelve days this process of offering went on.]

12 The one who brought his offering on the first day was Nahshon son of Amminadab of the tribe of Judah.

13 His offering was one silver plate weighing a hundred and thirty shekels, and one silver sprinkling bowl weighing seventy shekels, both according to the sanctuary shekel, each filled

Offering Is Part of Worship

with fine flour mixed with oil as a grain offering;

14 one gold dish weighing ten shekels, filled with incense [that would be worth thousands of dollars today];

15 one young bull, one ram and one male lamb a year old, for a burnt offering;

16 one male goat for a sin offering;

17 and two oxen, five rams, five male goats and five male lambs a year old, to be sacrificed as a fellowship offering. This was the offering of Nahshon son of Amminadab.

(Numbers 7:10–17)

God kept an absolute record of what each leader offered and then caused it to be preserved in Scripture in minute detail. We need to take note of the degree of importance God places on our offerings.

The New Testament teaches us that Jesus Himself watches how we give. We read in Mark 12:41–44:

41 Jesus sat down opposite the place where the offerings were put and watched the crowd putting their money into the temple treasury. Many rich people threw in large amounts.

42 But a poor widow came and put in two very small copper coins, worth only a fraction of a penny.

God's Plan for Your Money

⁴³ Calling his disciples to him, Jesus said, "I tell you the truth, this poor widow has put more into the treasury than all the others.

⁴⁴ They all gave out of their wealth; but she, out of her poverty, put in everything, all she had to live on."   (Mark 12:41–44)

Jesus thought it worthwhile to sit and watch what and how the people offered. He does the same today. We may not see Him, but He is watching how and what we give.

There are two important points here: first, Jesus looked at what everybody gave and estimated its true value; second, God gauges what we give by what we keep. Jesus stated that the one who put in the least in actual amount gave the most because she had nothing left. Bear in mind that when God measures what you give, He looks at what you retain for yourself.

One final point is that one day all of us will have to answer for ourselves to God:

¹² So then, each of us will give an account of himself to God.   (Romans 14:12)

That account lies ahead for every one of us. And the phrase in the original Greek, "to give account," is used primarily in reference to financial matters. So, every one of us is going to give a financial accounting to God.

How to Put God First

Chapter Four

How to Put God

FIRST

We have seen that God wants us to view our money as something holy. We mistakenly tend to think of money as something dirty or unworthy. However, money is a part of us. When we offer our money, we are offering a major part of ourselves to God. We need to offer our money in worship to God; our worship is complete only in this way.

We will now consider a simple way to put God first in handling our money that is both practical and scriptural. To honor God in our finances, we must first seek God's kingdom and His righteousness and then honor the Lord with our firstfruits. The key word is *first* all the way through. If we put money first rather than God, then we are idolaters.

A simple, practical, and scriptural way to put God first with your money is by consistently setting aside for God the first tenth of your income. This practice is traditionally known as "tithing." *Tithe* comes from an Old English word meaning "the tenth" and is used in the King James Version. Tithing is the regular practice of setting apart the first tenth of your total income for God. When you do that, you have laid a foundation for honoring God with your money.

Tithing goes back to Abraham. Some Christians think that tithing was first instituted under the Law of Moses, but that is incorrect. Tithing is at least four hundred years older than the law. Genesis 14:12–17 records that Abraham had just won a great battle over certain kings and that, in winning the battle, he had gathered a great quantity of booty. The narration continues,

> *18 Then Melchizedek king of Salem brought out bread and wine. He was priest of God Most High,*

> *19 and he blessed Abram, saying, "Blessed be Abram by God Most High, Creator of heaven and earth.*

How To Put God First

20 And blessed be God Most High, who delivered your enemies into your hand."
(Genesis 14:18–20)

Melchizedek was the priest of the Most High God, or God's representative in the earth at that particular time, and he blessed Abraham. How did Abraham respond? Abraham gave Melchizedek a tenth of everything he had gained in victory.

It is important to see that Abraham is presented in the New Testament as a father and a pattern to all subsequent believers. Romans 4:11–12 states:

11 So then, he [Abraham] *is the father of all who believe....*

12 And he is also the father of the circumcised who not only are circumcised but who also walk in the footsteps of the faith that our father Abraham had before he was circumcised [which was at the time Melchizedek met him].

In order to be children of Abraham, we must walk in the steps of Abraham's faith. This includes handling our money the way Abraham handled his money. In the fourth chapter of Romans, Paul continued:

16 Therefore, the promise comes by faith, so that it may be by grace and may be guaranteed to all Abraham's offspring—not only to those who

God's Plan for Your Money

are of the law but also to those who are of the faith of Abraham. He is the father of us all.
(Romans 4:16)

Abraham is our father when we walk in the footsteps of his faith. And when we develop the same kind of faith he had, we will acknowledge the areas of finances and material possessions as belonging to God, just as his faith did.

Now let us consider Jacob, Abraham's grandson. Jacob became a refugee because of the way he had tricked Isaac, his father, and Esau, his brother. He left the land of inheritance and went off to seek his fortune in Mesopotamia. When he set out, all he had in his hand was one staff. This is what Jacob said in Genesis 28:20–22:

> *20 Then Jacob made a vow, saying, "If God will be with me and will watch over me on this journey I am taking and will give me food to eat and clothes to wear*

> *21 so that I return safely to my father's house, then the LORD will be my God*

> *22 and this stone that I have set up as a pillar will be God's house, and of all that you give me I will give you a tenth."*

Here we find tithing again. In essence, Jacob said, "That's the basis of my relationship with God. He provides my needs, and in return, I give Him back a tenth of all that He provides for me."

How To Put God First

Then we read Jacob's testimony twenty years later.

> ⁹*Then Jacob prayed, "O God of my father Abraham, God of my father Isaac, O LORD, who said to me, 'Go back to your country and your relatives, and I will make you prosper'* [notice that key word *"prosper"*].
>
> ¹⁰*I am unworthy of all the kindness and faithfulness you have shown your servant. I had only my staff when I crossed this Jordan, but now I have become two groups."*
>
> (Genesis 32:9–10)

Jacob had tremendous wealth, a very large family, and every need had been supplied. What was the reason? His faithfulness in tithing. He left with one staff, and he came back with abundance. The key was that he gave God the first tenth of everything that God provided for him.

As we further examine tithing among God's people in the Old Testament, we find that under the Law of Moses, the tithe simply belonged to God. There was no question about this fact, which is verified in the following Scripture:

> ³⁰*A tithe of everything from the land, whether grain from the soil or fruit from the trees, belongs to the LORD; it is holy to the LORD* [the tithe is holy].
>
> ³² *The entire tithe of the herd and flock—every tenth animal that passes under the shepherd's rod—will be holy to the LORD.*
>
> (Leviticus 27:30, 32)

God's Plan for Your Money

The entire tithe is holy to the Lord. In Deuteronomy 14:22 God said: *"Be sure to set aside a tenth of all that your fields produce each year."* That is tithing.

Many Christians are not aware of this fact, but in the New Testament, tithing reappears in the priesthood of Jesus. Hebrews 6:19 speaks about *"the inner sanctuary behind the curtain,"* and the next verse tells us,

> *20 Jesus, who went before us, has entered on our behalf. He has become a high priest forever, in the order of Melchizedek.* (v. 6:20)

So Jesus is our High Priest in the order of Melchizedek.

In the next chapter of Hebrews, the writer explained the part tithing played in the priesthood of Melchizedek and in the high priesthood of Jesus:

> *4 Just think how great he* [Melchizedek] *was: even the patriarch Abraham gave him a tenth of the plunder!*
>
> *5 Now the law requires the descendants of Levi who become priests to collect a tenth from the people—that is, their brothers—even though their brothers are descended from Abraham.*
>
> *6 This man, however, did not trace his descent from Levi, yet he collected a tenth from Abraham and blessed him who had the promises.* [Notice the emphasis on the tenth.]

How To Put God First

⁷ And without doubt the lesser person is blessed by the greater. [Abraham was lesser than Melchizedek because he was blessed by Melchizedek.]

⁸ In the one case [the case of the law], *the tenth is collected by men who die; but in the other case, by him who is declared to be living.*
(Hebrews 7:4–8)

The priesthood of Melchizedek is an eternal priesthood because the one who is in the priesthood never dies. The writer stated that Jesus lives forever as a High Priest after the order of Melchizedek. And in His priesthood He receives the tithes of His people.

We can see that tithing has a continuous history from Abraham onwards: from Abraham to Jacob, to the nation of Israel, and then to the ministry of Jesus as our High Priest. According to Scripture, when we set aside our first tenth and offer our tithe to Jesus, we are actually acknowledging that Jesus is our High Priest according to the priesthood of Melchizedek. This is one of the ways we are able to honor Him and acknowledge Him as our High Priest.

God Challenges Us

Chapter Five

God Challenges Us

Now we will consider how God Himself actually challenges us to put Him to the test by following the scriptural examples of tithing. This complete challenge is given in Malachi when God was speaking to Israel:

> [7] *"Ever since the time of your forefathers you have turned away from my decrees and have not kept them. Return to me, and I will return to you," says the LORD Almighty. "But you ask, 'How are we to return?'*
>
> [8] *Will a man rob God? Yet you rob me. But you ask, 'How do we rob you?' In tithes and offerings."* (Malachi 3:7–8)

Notice that withholding God's appointed portion is called robbing God. Most of us would

God's Plan for Your Money

never rob another human being, but we might be guilty of robbing God.

God then told Israel the result of robbing Him and the remedy:

> ⁹*"You are under a curse—the whole nation of you—because you are robbing me.* [Now here is the remedy:]

> ¹⁰ *Bring the whole tithe into the storehouse, that there may be food in my house. Test me in this," says the LORD Almighty, "and see if I will not throw open the floodgates of heaven and pour out so much blessing that you will not have room enough for it."* (Malachi 3:9–10)

Upon what condition does God promise the blessing? When we bring the whole tithe into the storehouse. He says, "Test Me. See if I'll do what I've promised." God requires us to test Him with our finances; in other words, we must act in faith.

Finally, He goes on to speak of further results:

> ¹¹ *"I will prevent pests from devouring your crops, and the vines in your fields will not cast their fruit," says the LORD Almighty.*

> ¹² *"Then all the nations will call you blessed, for yours will be a delightful land," says the LORD Almighty.* (vv. 11–12)

God says that if you will honor Him in that way, then He will pour out such a blessing that

God Challenges Us

you will not find room to contain it. He will prevent the pests (the devourer) from eating up anything that is yours. All nations will look at you and say you are a blessed people and will recognize that God has truly blessed and prospered you. All this is promised as a result of bringing the whole tithe into the storehouse.

Let me summarize four points from this passage in Malachi:

1) For more than one thousand years, God kept a record of Israel's giving. He had required them to give the tithe to Him more than a thousand years earlier. Then at a certain point He told them He had kept a record, and they had been robbing Him. So, remember, God keeps a record.

2) Keeping back God's portion is robbery—not robbery of man, but robbery of God—and it brings a curse upon those who do it.

3) Faithful tithing brings a blessing, and through the results God is glorified in the blessing that comes on His people.

4) Tithing is a test of our faith and of God's faithfulness. But please take note: it must be done in faith.

Let us consider what the storehouse is in this passage. I want to illustrate this concept from the natural realm. A storehouse is basically two things: first, it is the place we get the food we eat; second, it is the place we obtain seed to sow for future harvests. As Christians, we receive our spiritual food from a certain source or sources, and we probably receive seed to sow in the lives of others from the same source. I suggest that wherever that source is for you is your storehouse and where you need to bring your tithe. If you belong to a local church that supplies those needs, then by all means that is your storehouse. Be faithful to tithe there. But many Christians today are not privileged in that way. They must consider what is the source of their food and the seed that is sown.

Let me share a little parable, which I will not seek to interpret. Normally, you do not eat in the Holiday Inn and pay your bill at Howard Johnson's. Meditate on this, and you will understand it for yourself.

Now, we must understand that tithing is not the end of giving to God, it is the beginning. Tithing lays a foundation for our systematic, continual giving to God. The Bible also speaks of giving in two other main categories: offerings and alms. We really do not offer our tithe to God, because it is His legal portion. But, beyond our tithe, what we give is offerings. Look at all the options Israel had for giving:

> [6]*Bring your burnt offerings and sacrifices, your tithes and special gifts, what you have*

God Challenges Us

*vowed to give and your freewill offerings, and
the firstborn of your herds and flocks.*
(Deuteronomy 12:6)

Six specific kinds of offerings are mentioned:

1) burnt offerings
2) sacrifices
3) special gifts
4) what you have vowed
5) freewill offerings
6) the firstborn of your herds and flocks

In other words, there is a very wide range of
different kinds of offerings that we can give to
God. But we do not offer our tithes; we simply
return to God that which is His scriptural portion.

In addition to offerings, there are what the
Bible calls "alms," or what is known today as
charity. This is not what we give to God, but what
we give to the needy, the poor and the afflicted.
The Bible has a lot more to say about giving to
the poor than many Christians have heard. This
is what Jesus said:

*[32] Do not be afraid, little flock, for your Father
has been pleased to give you the kingdom.*

*[33] Sell your possessions and give to the poor.
Provide purses for yourselves that will not
wear out, a treasure in heaven that will not be
exhausted, where no thief comes near and no
moth destroys.*

God's Plan for Your Money

*34 For where your treasure is, there your heart
will be also.*   (Luke 12:32–34)

Where you put your money is where your
heart is. You cannot have your money in one
place, your heart in another. Jesus said to act
like children of a king. Your Father has given you
the kingdom, so you can afford to be generous.
Give to the poor and lay up treasure for yourself
in heaven.

In Ecclesiastes 11:1–2 there is another mar-
velous picture of what we do when we give to the
poor:

> *1 Cast your bread upon the waters, for after
> many days you will find it again.*
>
> *2 Give portions to seven, yes to eight, for you
> do not know what disaster may come upon the
> land.*

I hope you can see that point. When you give
to the poor, then you are laying up insurance
with God. The writer said, *"Give to seven,"*—that's
your duty—*"and to eight,"*—go a little beyond
duty—*"because you do not know what disaster
might come upon the earth."* In other words, if you
do what God says with your money, God will take
care of you when the disaster comes. That is His
guarantee and that is your insurance. Giving is
an insurance against bad times.

Consider the testimony of Oswald J. Smith,
who was pastor of the People's Church in Toronto,

God Challenges Us

Canada, for many years. During the Great Depression, hundreds of men came to his office every day to ask for financial help from the church. He said they gave aid to hundreds, but that he always checked with each man whether that man had been faithful when he had an income to give the tithe to God. He reported that in all his experience, no man who came for help had ever been faithful in tithing. He concluded that God took care of all those who faithfully tithed.

The Grace of
Giving

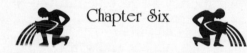 Chapter Six

The Grace of Giving

As we continue our study, we want to consider the spiritual key to the only kind of giving that is truly acceptable to God. It is expressed in one simple and beautiful word: *grace*. In the New Testament we are not talking about giving by law or commandment, but about giving that comes out of grace. Paul spokeabout this grace in the great giving chapter found in 2 Corinthians. Writing to the Christians in Corinth, he exhorted:

> *⁷But just as you excel in everything—in faith, in speech, in knowledge, in complete earnestness and in your love for us—see that you also excel in this grace of giving.*
>
> (2 Corinthians 8:7)

53

God's Plan for Your Money

The Corinthian church was well equipped with spiritual gifts and graces. It also had a good attitude of love. But Paul said, "Be sure you don't miss out on this other tremendously important grace, the grace of giving."

In this chapter that deals with giving, the word *grace* occurs seven times. It is the key word. Unless we understand grace and how grace motivates giving, we really cannot understand God's plan for our money as revealed in the New Testament.

The Bible speaks of both law and grace. Law is external, written on stone tablets in front of our eyes. It says, "Do this. Don't do that." But the law is not inside us, the old nature is. This rebel nature resists what is written on the tablets of the law outside.

However, grace is different. Grace is internal. It works from within, not from without. It is written on the heart, not on tablets of stone. It is written there only by the Holy Spirit. No other agent can write the grace of God in our hearts but the Holy Spirit. (See 2 Corinthians 3:3.)

We need to see how the New Testament contrasts law and grace. In John we read:

> [17] *For the law was given through Moses; grace and truth came through Jesus Christ.*
>
> (John 1:17)

The Grace of Giving

The law came through Moses, but grace comes only through Jesus Christ. If we want grace, it is made available to us only through Jesus Christ. Furthermore, it is made available only through the cross and what Jesus did on the cross. From the cross grace has been released and made available to the human race. This is true also in the area of finance. What Jesus did on the cross made provision for our prosperity:

> *⁹For you know the grace of our Lord Jesus Christ, that though he was rich, yet for your sakes he became poor, so that you through his poverty might become rich.*
>
> (2 Corinthians 8:9)

Notice the key word there at the beginning: *"grace."* It is not law; it is grace. We cannot earn it. Grace is manifested here in an exchange. Jesus was rich, but He became poor out of His grace in order that we, through His grace, being poor, might become rich with His riches. Jesus exhausted the poverty curse that results from the broken law so that, in return, through grace, we might receive the wealth of the kingdom of God. God's grace is through Jesus Christ and through the cross.

Also concerning grace, the New Testament reveals that grace is received only through faith. The very essence of grace is that it cannot be earned. There is nothing we can ever do that will deserve the grace of God. Paul said this in Ephesians:

> *⁸For it is by grace you have been saved, through faith—and this not from yourselves, it is the gift of God—*
>
> *⁹ not by works, so that no one can boast.*
>
> (Ephesians 2:8–9)

Notice the order: *"by grace"*—*"through faith"*—*"not by works."* I am not teaching you about a plan by which you can earn your money. I am teaching about something that you can receive only by grace through faith. In Galatians, Paul said:

> *⁶For in Christ Jesus neither circumcision nor uncircumcision means anything, but faith working through love.* (Galatians 5:6 NAS)

Faith is the only way we can appropriate the grace of God. The faith that appropriates God's grace works by love. This is the spiritual key to right giving. I want to state it very clearly:

> The spiritual key to right giving is grace (not law) received through Jesus and through the cross by faith, and working by love.

I want to emphasize that the Bible's principles of finance, as unfolded in the New Testament, can only be apprehended by faith. You must respond to this message with faith. Further, faith means that we act. Faith without actions is dead. What do we do? We give. We give before we have received. This is contrary to the thinking of the carnal mind. The carnal mind says, "I can't afford to give." Faith says, "You can't afford not to give because that is the key to receiving." In Luke, Jesus said:

> 38 *Give, and it will be given to you; good measure, pressed down, shaken together, running over, they will pour into your lap. For by your standard of measure it will be measured to you in return.* (Luke 6:38 NASB)

What happens first? Do we receive, or do we give? We give. Give, and it will be given back. We give to God, and God causes men to give back to us. That is God's control over the situation.

Then Jesus brought out this second principle: "Whatever measure you deal out to others, it will be dealt to you in return." If you want to receive generously, then Jesus said you have to give generously.

That truth is remarkable. In actual fact, you have the key to your financial prosperity in your hands. It is the key of faith, responding to God's grace. You can do two things. First, you can take the initiative by giving. You do not have to wait, you can give. Second, you can set the proportion that you wish to receive, because the proportion that you give determines the proportion that you receive. You do not have to sit passively wishing or hoping. You can begin to act in faith with your finances according to God's revealed plan in the New Testament. When you do this, your finances then become God's responsibility.

First Give Yourself

Chapter Seven

First Give Yourself

Our next Scripture comes from the eighth chapter of 2 Corinthians. I suggest that you take time to read chapters eight and nine through several times with careful consideration to get the full impact of the passage. The entire theme of both chapters is finances. Whoever said the Bible does not have much to say about money?

Paul was writing to the Corinthians about the Macedonian churches, and he was telling how the Holy Spirit moved on the Macedonians to be generous in their giving. Then he drew a lesson from that. In 2 Corinthians 8:2–5, we read:

God's Plan for Your Money

² Out of the most severe trial, their over-flowing joy [the Macedonian churches] *and their extreme poverty welled up in rich gener-osity.*

³ For I testify that they gave as much as they were able, and even beyond their ability. Entirely on their own,

⁴ they urgently pleaded with us for the privilege of sharing in this service to the saints.

⁵ And they did not do as we expected, but they gave themselves first to the Lord and then to us in keeping with God's will.

(2 Corinthians 8:2–5)

The important sentence here is, *"They gave themselves first to the Lord."* What is the first thing we have to give to the Lord? Not our money, but ourselves. That is how it must begin with each of us. Do not give your money to God if you have not given yourself. You must begin with yourself. You cannot buy a good relation-ship with God. Actually, God can get on all right without your money. It is for your benefit that God requires you to give, but He has an order. He wants you first. Then, out of the giving of yourself, by His grace, the kind of giving the New Testament talks about will naturally flow.

In Romans 12:1–2, we see this same princi-ple:

First Give Yourself

¹ Therefore, I urge you, brothers, in view of God's mercy, to offer your bodies as living sacrifices, holy and pleasing to God—this is your spiritual act of worship.

² Do not conform any longer to the pattern of this world, but be transformed by the renewing of your mind. Then you will be able to test and approve what God's will is—his good, pleasing and perfect will. (Romans 12:1–2)

The key to finding God's will, and that includes God's will for your money, is offering yourself as a living sacrifice. That means making yourself totally and unreservedly available to God for His service. When you do that, your mind is renewed by the Holy Spirit, and you begin to think a different way. As you begin to think differently, then you can find God's will in its three successive phases: *"good, pleasing and perfect."* Then, as you find God's will, you should begin to discover that God's plan for your money is included in His will. God's plan for your life covers every facet of living.

Nothing exists for which He has not made provision and for which He does not accept responsibility. But you must meet Him on His terms. Do not start by giving your money; start by giving yourself. Present yourself and all that you are to the Lord as a living sacrifice on the altar of His service. Then your mind will begin to grasp the fullness of God's provision and plan for you.

God's Plan for Your Money

I have walked in this way for more than forty years, and I want you to know that there are still many areas of God's perfect will for my life into which I have not fully entered. But, as far as finances are concerned, I have applied the principles I am sharing with you to my own life and can testify that they work.

Once we have given ourselves to God, the giving of our money (or whatever other gifts we may offer to God) completes and establishes our righteousness. It is very important to see that what you do with your money can establish you forever in God's righteousness. In 2 Corinthians, Paul quoted from the book of Psalms in the Old Testament:

> [9]As it is written "He has scattered abroad his gifts to the poor; his righteousness endures forever." (2 Corinthians 9:9)

Notice the order: the righteous man first gives himself to God and then gives liberally to others. It is said of him, *"His righteousness endures forever."* His giving of his money establishes him forever in the righteousness of God.

I would like to quote from the psalm that Paul quoted:

> [1]Blessed is the man who fears the LORD, who finds great delight in his commands.

[That includes His commands concerning money.]

First Give Yourself

³ Wealth and riches are in his house, and his righteousness endures forever.

⁴ Even in darkness light dawns for the upright, for the gracious and compassionate and righteous man.

⁵ Good will come to him who is generous and lends freely, who conducts his affairs with justice.

⁶ Surely he will never be shaken; a righteous man will be remembered forever.

[The key to this unshakable righteousness is handling your finances rightly, graciously, with compassion and generosity.]

⁹ He has scattered abroad his gifts to the poor, his righteousness endures forever.

(Psalm 112:1, 3–6, 9)

The theme of this psalm is that right dealing with our finances establishes us forever in the righteousness of God. I think the converse is also obviously true. If we do not handle our money rightly, we will never be established in the righteousness of God. The way we handle our money is very decisive.

Let me give you a beautiful teaching of Jesus found in Matthew:

¹⁹ Do not store up for yourselves treasures on earth, where moth and rust destroy, and where thieves break in and steal.

God's Plan for Your Money

20 But store up for yourselves treasures in heaven, where moth and rust do not destroy, and where thieves do not break in and steal.

21 For where your treasure is, there your heart will be also. (Matthew 6:19–21)

Right giving insures that God will provide for us in this world, but that is not the ultimate. The ultimate truth is that we are laying up treasure in heaven in proportion to what we give on earth.

Our provision is on earth, but
our treasure is in heaven.

Where you invest is where you are concerned. If you want to be more concerned for the kingdom of God and if you want to have a greater zeal for the things of God, then I will tell you one way to achieve that end: invest more. The more you invest, the more concerned you will be. *"Where your treasure is, there your heart will be also"* (Matthew 6:21).

A Two-Way
Relationship

Chapter Eight

A Two-Way Relationship

Remember that the first gift we need to give to God is ourselves. We cannot offer God anything that is acceptable to Him until we have offered ourselves. However, once we have truly given ourselves to God, as Paul describes in Romans 12, whatever we give in faith completes and establishes our righteousness. Paul quotes Psalm 112:9 in this connection when he spoke about a certain righteous man: *"He has scattered abroad his gifts to the poor, his righteousness endures forever."* In fact, the theme of Psalm 112 is how generosity and compassion and right giving establish enduring righteousness that will never be eliminated.

God's Plan for Your Money

We will now consider giving as a two-way relationship between God and the giver. First, let us consider giving as a proof of our love for God. In 2 Corinthians 8:7–8, we find the following:

> *⁷ But just as you excel in everything—in faith, in speech, in knowledge, in complete earnestness and in your love for us—see that you also excel in this grace of giving.*
>
> *⁸ I am not commanding you, but I want to test the sincerity of your love by comparing it with the earnestness of others.*

A complete Christian, or a complete Christian church, must be able to excel in the *"grace of giving."* Paul emphasized that this is not law, but rather grace.

Paul had been speaking to the Corinthians about the generosity of the Macedonian Christians. Then he said, "Now I want to see if your love is really sincere, and I'll find out by measuring what you give with what the Macedonian Christians gave." That is pretty plain talk. Paul sincerely loved the Corinthian Christians. They were his spiritual children and the fruit of his ministry. But here he said that he wants to find out whether their love for God was sincere or whether it was just talk, and that the way he could find out is by seeing how much they gave. The standard with which he would compare them was the Macedonian Christians, who gave with amazing generosity out of their poverty. The

A Two-Way Relationship

Macedonians had proven their love. Now Paul was telling the Corinthians, "The ball is in your court. How about you? How are you going to respond to this challenge to prove your love for God?"

A little further on in the same chapter, Paul said:

> ²⁴ *Therefore show these men* [the representatives of the churches who had come] *the proof of your love and the reason for our pride in you, so that the churches can see it.*
> (2 Corinthians 8:24)

Some people's giving is so secret that nobody knows about it. I wonder if it is secret because they would be embarrassed if anybody did know. But Paul said that giving to God does not have to be done in secret. He told the Corinthians to do it in front of everybody. They were to let everybody see their commitment to the Lord. He had boasted about them, had been proud of them, and it was very important to him that they prove their love in this vital matter of giving.

Our giving proves our love for God as well as for our fellow believers. This truth was very plainly stated by the apostle John in 1 John 3:16–18:

> ¹⁶ *This is how we know what love is: Jesus Christ laid down his life for us. And we ought*

to lay down our lives for our brothers. [We ought to do to others as Jesus did for us.]

[17] If anyone has material possessions and sees his brother in need but has no pity on him, how can the love of God be in him?

[18] Dear children, let us not love with words or tongue but with actions and in truth.
(1 John 3:16–18)

Laying down our lives for our brothers includes helping them with our material resources if they are in need and we are in a position to help. There is a saying in our contemporary culture that I think is pretty good: "Put your money where your mouth is." That is exactly what John was saying. He said, "You've said it, now do it! Don't love just with words and in tongue, *'but with actions and in truth.'*"

John continued with an amazing statement about love in action:

[19] This then is how we know that we belong to the truth, and how we set our hearts at rest in his presence

[20] whenever our hearts condemn us. For God is greater than our hearts, and he knows everything.
(1 John 3:19–20)

So, if we are feeling condemned and wondering whether we are accepted with God, John said our generosity will set our hearts at rest.

A Two-Way Relationship

That is exactly what Paul was saying when he was quoted Psalm 112:9: *"He has scattered abroad his gifts to the poor, his righteousness endures forever."*

We have two alternatives when it comes to love: one is to love just in words and in tongue; the other is to love in actions and in truth. One of the ways to answer that challenge is by what we do with our finances. We will prove whether our love is just in word and in tongue, or whether it is in action and in truth, by the measure of our generosity.

As I have already stated, giving to God is a two-way relationship. The first aspect of the relationship is our attitude to God. We prove our love for God by giving to Him.

The second aspect of the relationship is God's response to us. The New Testament teaches that right giving is a cause of God's special love for us. God loves the world, but He loves some people in a special way. One class of people He loves specially are those who give generously and happily:

> *[7] Each man should give what he has decided in his heart to give, not reluctantly or under compulsion, for God loves a cheerful giver.*
> (2 Corinthians 9:7)

Do you want to be loved by God? One way is to give cheerfully. *"God loves a cheerful giver."*

God's Plan for Your Money

The Greek word that is translated *"cheerful"* is the word from which we derive the English word *hilarious*. God loves a hilarious giver. Have you ever thought of giving with hilarity?

Having spent five years in East Africa, I can remember scenes in African churches where the people gave with hilarity. By our American standards they were extremely poor. Most did not have money, but they would give in kind: coffee beans, corn, eggs, or chickens.

I remember seeing the African women walking up to the front of the church with a couple of ears of corn or even a live chicken balanced on top of their heads. (They carried everything on top of their heads.) They would put their gifts down at the altar, go back, be touched by God again, and come running up with another gift. I do not think I have ever seen people happier than those simple people. They were hilarious givers.

Why should people be hilarious when they give? Let me give you three reasons:

• First, giving is the supernatural grace of the Holy Spirit. Remember, giving is grace, not law. The Holy Spirit is the Spirit of Grace, and when we line ourselves up with what the Holy Spirit can bless, He comes upon us with supernatural grace. When He does, we get happy in a way we cannot be happy in the natural realm.

A Two-Way Relationship

• Second, giving calls down God's favor on us. The Bible says God's favor is like a *"shield"* (Psalm 84:11) and like *"a cloud of the latter rain"* (Proverbs 16:15 KJV). Giving is the catalyst for the precipitation of His bless ings upon us.

• Third, hilarious giving releases us from slavery to "mammon." Mammon is that evil, satanic power that enslaves men and women through money. When we begin to give hilariously, we are saying to mammon, "Away with you. You're not going to dictate to me. You're not going to dominate my thinking. I'm going to give with joy because I'm giving to God, and God loves a cheerful giver."

Giving Is Sowing

Chapter Nine

Giving Is Sowing

Another aspect of giving is sowing seed. In 2 Corinthians 9:6–7, Paul said this:

> *⁶ Remember this: Whoever sows sparingly will also reap sparingly, and whoever sows generously will also reap generously.*
>
> *⁷ Each man should give what he has decided in his heart to give.*

In talking about giving our money, Paul used the metaphorical figure of sowing and reaping. This analogy is taken from agriculture, but he is not talking about a farmer and his farm. He is talking about the Christian and his giving to God and the kingdom of God.

Certain basic principles of agriculture must be followed if you want to succeed in agriculture. The possibility of success exists, but achieving success depends upon your following the principles or laws of agriculture.

When we think of giving as sowing (in agricultural terms), we understand that we should expect an increase from our giving, but only in proportion to what we sow. For example, when sowing seed a farmer sows one bushel of wheat. When harvested, his wheat crop yields a biblical proportion, a hundredfold increase. By that proportion of increase, he receives one hundred bushels of wheat. That is an easy calculation. If he sows ten bushels and his proportionate increase is one hundred times the amount sown, he receives one thousand bushels. In other words, the original investment of seed sown determines the amount that is harvested or reaped. Paul says the same is true with giving money to God and His kingdom.

Let me give a simple example: A person gives five dollars. The proportion of increase is ten. What is he going to receive back? Fifty dollars. If he gives fifty dollars, and the proportion of increase is the same, he is going to get back five hundred dollars. The degree of generosity with which he gives determines the proportionate size of the return that he will receive back.

Giving Is Sowing

Almost everybody can understand the principle of proportion in agriculture, but so few people understand it in the finances of the kingdom of God. The Bible makes it very clear that the same kinds of laws that apply in agriculture also apply in the finances of the kingdom of God. This is a principle of sowing and of reaping.

In order to obtain the increase, a farmer must follow certain basic rules. I would suggest that the following non-exhaustive guidelines that are employed in agriculture are also applicable in the area of giving:

1) The farmer must choose good, suitable soil and the right kind of crop for the right kind of soil.

2) He must make proper preparation of the soil.

3) He must take proper care of the crop as it grows.

If he does not meet these conditions, he will not receive the increase that he ought to receive. His failure to receive will not be because there is anything wrong with the laws of agriculture, but because he has not applied some of the basic rules.

A farmer does not walk down the street of the town casting his seed into the gutter on either side of the street and then expect a harvest. You might say that idea is absurd. But I have observed many Christians doing something that is analogous to this with their money. They cast it away without care or prayer in places where it will never bring an increase. Then they wonder why God does not bless their finances.

We need to follow certain basic rules that are just like the basic principles the farmer follows. We do not sow in the gutter; we choose good soil. We make sure the soil is properly prepared, and we try to see that care is taken of the crop as it grows.

What are the things that we should look at when we consider giving to a church or a ministry or an organization? I will give you four questions that I think you need to ask:

1) Is the ministry anointed and fruitful? Is it bringing forth real fruit for the kingdom of God?

2) Is it ethical? Is it ethical in the way it appeals for money? Is it ethical in the way it handles money? Is it a good and faithful steward of the money in God's kingdom?

3) Is it aligned with Scripture? Is what it is doing in obedience to scriptural principles? This point is very important, because God blesses what is in line with His Word.

4) Are the leaders prayerful, industrious, and efficient? The Bible makes it very clear that

Giving Is Sowing

God hates sloppiness, waste, and extravagance. That does not mean we have to be stingy, but it does mean we cannot afford to be extravagant, and we should not support extravagance in any ministry.

I would like to offer you some other practical safeguards in connection with investing your money in the kingdom of God. When people of this world invest their money, they like to get good advice from someone who is proficient in investments. I think God's children should be equally careful in their own way. Let me give you four safeguards for investing:

1) Be prayerful. Never give except after prayer.

2) Avoid impulsive, emotional giving. I have seen countless sums of money squandered by people who gave out of emotion and impulse. There are people going around deliberately exploiting God's people to get money. There is no group of people in the world easier to exploit than American Christians. They are generous but, frankly, they are often impulsive.

3) Maintain contact with whatever individual or organization you are supporting. Get reports. Find out what is happening. Check on the fruit.

4) Stay within the proportion of your faith. Allow God to increase your faith in a natural

God's Plan for Your Money

way. If you are accustomed to thinking in terms of ten dollars, it is probably unrealistic to think immediately in terms of one thousand dollars. Faith grows in a natural way. If you have been thinking in terms of ten dollars, progress to fifty. When you are comfortable with fifty, then move up to a hundred.

Finally, there are four results of wise sowing of your money. They were stated by Paul in 2 Corinthians:

> [10]*Now he* [God] *who supplies seed to the sower and bread for food will also supply and increase your store of seed and will enlarge the harvest of your righteousness.*
> (2 Corinthians 9:10)

The four results of wise sowing are:

1) Bread for you to eat. You will get back all that you need for your own life.

2) You will get more seed to sow in God's harvest field. If you have been giving fifty dollars, you will find that you can move up to one hundred dollars. That is seed to sow back into God's harvest field, not to squander on your own selfishness.

3) You will get increased store for sowing. Your barn will get bigger. You will have more to give.

Giving Is Sowing

4) You will get an increased harvest from increased sowing. 2 Corinthians 9:10 says, "[God] *will enlarge the harvest of your righteousness.*"

I want to tell you that learning to give prayerfully, in a scriptural way, and in the guidance of the Holy Spirit is exciting, not a dreary duty. It is exciting to see how God will come to your help and extend and increase your faith. God wants you to invest in His kingdom. If you will seek God's counsel, He will make you a successful investor.

God's Level Is
Abundance

 Chapter Ten

God's Level Is Abundance

T hus far, we have established six important facts in connection with giving. First, the key to right giving is grace. Grace comes only through Jesus, through the cross, and is received only by faith.

Second, we must first give ourselves. We cannot buy God's favor. He requires that we first surrender ourselves to Him before our gifts can become acceptable.

Third, giving completes and establishes our righteousness.

God's Plan for Your Money

Fourth, giving is a proof of the sincerity of our love, both for God and for our fellow believers.

Fifth, giving calls down God's favor and love upon us. God loves a hilarious giver.

Sixth, giving is sowing in God's harvest field. The same principles that apply to agriculture apply to giving. The Lord wants us to understand and employ these principles so that we may be blessed, we may have enough food for ourselves, we may have seed to sow, our barns for storage may be enlarged, and our harvest may increase.

Finally, we need to see that the level of God's provision for His people is abundance. One of the most powerful verses in the New Testament states this truth:

> *8 And God is able to make all grace abound to you, so that in all things at all times, having all that you need, you will abound in every good work.* (2 Corinthians 9:8)

Again, notice it is by grace—not by law. The principle of grace is stated in 2 Corinthians 8:9:

> *9 For you know the grace of our Lord Jesus Christ, that though he was rich, yet for your sakes he became poor, so that you through his poverty might become rich.*
> (2 Corinthians 8:9)

God's Level Is Abundance

You need to keep these two references in your mind: 2 Corinthians 8:9 and 2 Corinthians 9:8. The first speaks about the grace of the Lord Jesus Christ, that on the cross He became poor with our poverty so that we might by faith share His riches. In the second one Paul told us the level of the grace that is released to us through the cross:

> *8 God is able to make all grace abound to you, so that in all things at all times, having all that you need, you will abound in every good work.*
> (2 Corinthians 9:8)

If you analyze the latter verse, you will find two key words: the word *"abound"* and the word *"all." "Abound"* occurs twice and *"all"*—or *"every"*—occurs five times in that one verse. In no way could the language be more emphatic. When speaking about the level of God's provision for His people, it says, *"**All** grace...so that in **all** things at **all** times, having **all** that you need, you will abound in **every** good work."* (The last word in English is *"every,"* but in the Greek it is the same word as for *"all."*) If you have all that you need in all things at all times to abound to every good work, there is absolutely no room for unsupplied need anywhere in your life.

Let us consider for a moment the meaning of abundance. From its Latin origin, the word *abundance* speaks of "a wave that overflows." Your swimming pool has abundance when it overflows. Your sink has abundance when it spills over. A thing has no abundance until it overflows.

God's Plan for Your Money

Jesus said, *"Out of the abundance of the heart, the mouth speaks"* (Matthew 12:34 NKJV). When your heart overflows, it overflows through your mouth.

What does it mean to have overflowing provision? Let me illustrate this concept very simply. You need $50 worth of groceries, but you have only $40. So when you go to the grocery store, you are shopping out of insufficiency. If you have $50 and you need $50 worth of groceries, you are shopping out of sufficiency. You have just enough. But if you need $50 worth of groceries and you go to the store with $60, you are shopping out of abundance. You have more than enough; there is an overflow.

God's provision is on that level. God does not merely offer us just enough. If we, by faith, appropriate His grace, then the level of His provision is abundance. We have more than enough for all our needs and for ourselves.

You need to take notice that the final purpose of abundance is *"every good work"* (2 Corinthians 9:8). It is not selfish indulgence; it is being able to do good works.

Why does God want His children to have abundance? His specific, practical reason is contained in Acts, where Paul was quoting Jesus:

> [35]*The Lord Jesus himself said: "It is more blessed to give than to receive."* (Acts 20:35)

God's Level Is Abundance

Receiving has a blessing, but giving has a greater blessing. God has no favorites among His children. He wants all His children to enjoy the greater blessing of giving. God makes His abundance available to us so that we may not be limited to the blessing of receiving, but that we may also be in a position to enjoy the greater blessing of giving.

To complete what I have been teaching about giving, I want to add a word of warning. If you want to enter into what I have been teaching, you will have to express your faith in action. It will not be enough just to give mental assent to what I am saying. You cannot merely say, "Well, that was good teaching. Isn't that wonderful! God wants me to prosper. He wants me to have abundance." Nothing will change in your life if you go no further than that. At some point, you must express this teaching, if you believe it, in your actions by faith.

James 2:26 says, *"As the body without the spirit is dead, so faith without deeds* [or actions] *is dead."* You can believe everything but still have nothing if you don't add action to your faith. You must act in faith.

If you want this kind of abundance, which comes by grace, not by law, then you must act in faith, and that means you must give first. The words of Jesus in Luke 6:38 express this idea:

> [38] *Give, and it will be given to you. A good measure, pressed down, shaken together and*

running over, will be poured into your lap. For
with the measure you use, it will be measured
to you. (Luke 6:28)

Do you want a *"good measure"* to be given to
you? Then you must give first. That is faith. If you
are not willing to act in faith, you will not set in
motion the processes that will bring God's prosperity and God's abundance into your life.

We need to bear in mind that usually a time
interval between sowing and reaping occurs. The
farmer does not sow one day and reap the next.
He first has to let the seed fall into the ground
and apparently die. Then, when it has fallen into
the ground and died, the harvest comes up. This
important lesson was expressed by Paul:

⁹Let us not become weary in doing good [and
that includes doing good with our money], *for*
at the proper time we will reap a harvest if we
do not give up. (Galatians 6:9)

Paul was saying in this passage that we must
wait for God's appointed time for the harvest. It
will come if we do not give up. But if we become
impatient or lose our faith or turn away from
these principles, then God does not guarantee
the harvest. We must live and act in faith in every
area of our lives, including our money.

About the Author

Derek Prince was born in India of British parents. He was educated as a scholar of Greek and Latin at Eton College and Cambridge University, England, where he held a Fellowship in Ancient and Modern Philosophy at King's College. He also studied Hebrew and Aramaic, both at Cambridge University and the Hebrew University in Jerusalem. In addition, he speaks a number of other modern languages. While serving with the British army in World War II, he began to study the Bible and experienced a life-changing encounter with Jesus Christ. Out of this encounter he formed two conclusions: first, that Jesus Christ is alive; second, that the Bible is a true, relevant, up-to-date book. These conclusions altered the whole course of his life. Since then, he has devoted his life to studying and teaching the Bible. His daily radio broadcast, *Keys to Successful Living,* reaches more than half the world and includes translations into Aramaic, Chinese, Croation, Malagasy, Mongolian, Russian, Samoan, Spanish, and Tongan. He is the author of over 50 books, over 500 audio and 160 video teaching cassettes, many of which have been translated and published in more than 60 languages.

Derek's main gift is explaining the Bible and its teachings in a clear and simple way. His non-denominational, non-sectarian approach has made his teaching equally relevant and helpful to people from all racial and religious backgrounds.